Let's Wonder About Science

THE ATOMS FAMILY

J.M. Patten, Ed.D.

The Rourke Book Co., Inc.
Vero Beach, Florida 32964

S

PHOTO CREDITS
All photos © J.M. Patten

Library of Congress Cataloging-in-Publication Data

Patten, J.M., 1944-
    The atoms' family / J.M. Patten.
    p. cm. — (Let's wonder about science)
    Includes index.
    ISBN 1-55916-125-6
    1. Atoms—Juvenile literature. [1. Atoms.] I. Title. II. Series:
Patten, J.M., 1944- Let's wonder about science.
QC173.36.P38 1995
539'.1—dc20
                             94-47598
                                CIP
                             AC r95

Printed in the USA

TABLE OF CONTENTS

WHAT IS SCIENCE?

Welcome to the story of **atoms.** They are an important part of science because they are what trees, mountains and people are made of.

The atoms family is amazing. There are more than 100 family members. However, they don't live inside a house or an apartment, eat pizza or play games like your family.

Atoms are tiny, tiny bits of nature that come together in special ways. Atoms make everything in the world.

Let's meet the atoms family and read all about them.

All the parts of this screen and the climbing caterpillar are made of atoms.

WHAT IS AN ATOM?

What is an atom? To find out, let's wonder about what all things are really made of.

What makes an ant an ant? You know about its parts—a mouth, eyes and feet. What is the very smallest part of an ant's eye or foot? The smallest part is an atom, of course!

An atom is the smallest part of this beautiful South American butterfly.

Pancakes, dishes, chairs, tables, knives, forks and this book are all made of tiny particles called atoms.

An atom is the smallest part of any living or nonliving thing that takes up space. Ants, trees, water, air and even you are made of tiny **particles** called atoms. Atoms are the "building blocks" that make up everything.

HOW SMALL IS AN ATOM?

Atoms are very, very, very small. How small? Over 250 billion atoms fit on the point of a pencil.

People cannot see atoms with a magnifying glass or even the strongest regular microscope. Scientists look at atoms with special **electron microscopes.**

An electron microscope is so large it fills a whole room. Only a highly-trained scientist can use this expensive scientific instrument.

Atoms are very small. Over 250 billion atoms fit easily on the very tip on this pencil point.

PEOPLE FIND OUT ABOUT ATOMS

Two thousand years ago, people asked this question—what is the smallest part of anything? They really wondered and thought hard about this.

Early scientists did not have fancy microscopes. The powerful tools they used were their eyes to look and their brains to think.

Long ago these scientists gathered information and made **observations.** They looked and they thought. In this way they concluded, or decided, everything must be made of tiny, tiny particles. They called these particles atoms.

This magnifying glass makes the pen look larger. Atoms are so small they can only be seen with electron microscopes.

EARLY SCIENTISTS AND THE SCIENTIST IN YOU

The scientist in you makes observations and comes to **conclusions** all the time. For example, think about this. At the store, you see a man with a big bag of dog food in his shopping cart. You reach a conclusion—that man has a dog.

Observe, or look, at Helping Harry. Did you conclude, or figure out, that Harry is helpful because he has lots of hands?

Only an electron microscope can show the tiny atoms this girl and all people, plants and animals are made of.

Did you see the dog or pet the dog? No, but you made a very good guess based on what you could see.

That's just what those scientists from long ago did. They could not observe the tiny particles, but they concluded all things were made up of atoms.

ATOMS MAKE EVERYTHING

Ice, tomatoes, clothes, cars, dogs, cats, ants, lions, flowers, dirt, french fries, pizza, soda pop, grandma, baseballs, chairs, soap, sand, water—everything that takes up space is made from atoms. Even though they are very small, atoms have a big job.

Different kinds of atoms join together to make different things. Some make trees, some make water and some make you.

The mailbox and grass are made up of tiny particles called atoms.

THE ATOMS FAMILY

Today scientists know there are about 100 different kinds of atoms at work—like 100 different puzzle pieces.

Some members of the atoms family you might know are hydrogen, oxygen, sodium, aluminum, sulfur, calcium, iron, lead, copper, gold and silver.

It takes billions of silver atoms to make one tiny speck of silver. Atoms are so small, it takes billions of them to make anything at all.

Billions of silver atoms are needed to make just a speck of silver in this coin.

BUILDING BLOCKS

Atoms are called the "building blocks" of all things. Do you play with those plastic blocks that hook together?

Make believe these blocks are atoms. Make a house. Then, take the blocks apart and make a bridge.

The little red wagon has parts made from wood, metal and rubber. All the parts are made of atoms.

This model house was built with blocks that lock together. Atoms are the building blocks of all things.

First you made one thing. Then, you put the blocks together a different way to make something else.

Atoms work somewhat like plastic building blocks. If you put them together one way, they make a certain thing. If you put them together another way, they make a different thing.

ATOMS TO MOLECULES

Two or more atoms that are joined together are called **molecules.** Some molecules have one kind of atom in them. Most have more.

Let's make a molecule. Take two hydrogen atoms, add one oxygen atom, and you have a molecule of water—the famous H_2O.

It's amazing when you think of it. The water you swim in is made of hydrogen and oxygen atoms joined together. Science can be the best kind of magic.

These friends join together to make a two-headed person like atoms join together to make molecules.

GLOSSARY

atom (A tum) — the smallest part of any living or nonliving thing

conclusion (kun KLOO jhun) — in science, a decision based on observation

electron microscope (eh LEK trahn MY kreh skohp) — a powerful instrument used to look at atoms

molecule (MAHL eh kyool) — tiny particles formed by two or more different kinds of atoms joined together

observation (ahb zer VAY shun) — in science, observation is looking at things to find out how they work

particle (PART i kuhl) — something very tiny; atoms are sometimes called particles

The water we drink or play in is made from two kinds of atoms—hydrogen and oxygen.

INDEX